Love
Live &
Share

December 1980

*This book expresses my
many feelings about
you, me and us.*

*Love,
Elizabeth*

Other books by

Susan Polis Schutz

Come Into the Mountains, Dear Friend
I Want to Laugh, I Want to Cry
Peace Flows from the Sky
Someone Else to Love
I'm Not That Kind of Girl
Yours If You Ask

Love
Live &
Share

By

Susan Polis Schutz

Designed and illustrated by

Stephen Schutz

Blue Mountain Press ™

Boulder, Colorado

Acknowledgments:

"I never knew how it felt," "When you are gone,"
Copyright © Continental Publications, 1978.
"When we met," "I will support you," "Why do I put you,"
"Words are so inadequate," "I want to walk," "I am not
always happy," "We need to grow," "My trust for you,"
"Children everywhere," "You had to go," "After ten years,"
"In order to have," "Let us grow together," "Where there is
honesty," "Times have changed," "Everyone is running,"
"Where are all the people," "Many people," "When we
lived," "Everyone searches," "I will fill," "Though we are,"
"When I am down," "I want to be able to," Copyright ©
Continental Publications, 1979. All rights reserved.

Library of Congress Number: 80-66672
ISBN: 0-88396-118-0

Manufactured in the United States of America
First Printing: October, 1980

Blue Mountain Press INC

P.O. Box 4549, Boulder, Colorado 80306

CONTENTS

INTRODUCTION

Stephen and I have come to realize that no matter what
we search for, or what we achieve, it is the sharing of our
lives with those we love that really makes us happy.
In the last two and one-half years since I wrote **Yours If You
Ask**, I have spent most of my time with my family as
physically removed from the "hubbub" of career-oriented
pressure as I could possibly be. We lived a life-style best
suited for us. We hiked in the mountains, swam in the
ocean, wrote and illustrated **Love, Live and Share** and
worked on many interesting projects as we looked forward
to having a new baby.

I believe that most of the poems in this book reflect our
retreat from society to more spiritual and mystical things.

I am always so happy to hear that people relate
to my poems. I continually hope that I am growing with
and relating to you.

Love
      Live and
            Share

Susan Polis Schutz

P. S. Again and again, thank you for listening.

I am overwhelmed
with you and
the love we share

When we met
I was overwhelmed with the
idea of
you
When we got to know each other
I learned that you were a person
with strengths and weaknesses
  like everyone else
When we got closer
I was overwhelmed with the
idea of
love
Now that time has passed
I am no longer overwhelmed
with the idea of you and love
but I am more than overwhelmed
with you and the love we share

I will support you
in all that you
do
I will help you
in all that you
need
I will share with you
in all that you
experience
I will encourage you
in all that you
try
I will understand you
in all that is in your
heart
I will love you
in all that you
are

I never knew how it felt
to be alone
until you went away
so alone
I tried doing the things we did together
but they only reminded me of you
I tried doing things we did not do
but I couldn't get involved in anything
I tried smiling
but tears were always in my eyes
I tried laughing
but nothing was funny
so alone
I never knew how it felt
to be alone
until you went away
I never knew how it felt to love
until you came back

Words are so
inadequate to
express the overwhelming
sense of feelings
I have
for you—
I feel excited
and elated
I feel strong
and confident
I feel stable
and warm
Though I can't really
explain how
I feel
I do know that
I am very happy
inside
Thank you

I am not always
happy
There are so
many things
that make me
sad
that make me
furious
that make me ready to
explode
But our beautiful
relationship
is what keeps
me from concentrating
on these things and
enables me
to enjoy the
good
in
life

 I
want to
walk and feel the hot
sand on my skin
I want to
run and have the misty
breeze blow through my hair
I want to
swim and have the waves
sweep me to the shore
I want to
watch the bright red sun
fade into the ocean
and then I want to
join you
and help the stars reach the sky
as we create a sunburst
I want to
warm the entire dark land
with our fire
I want to
hold on to you tightly while I sleep
and dream about the dancing clouds
and then I want to
join you again
and wake up
the entire land
with our screams
I want to help
the sun rise
as we celebrate
another beautiful
morning
together

When you are gone
tears come to my eyes
when I look at the ocean
when I pick flowers
when I go to sleep
I don't think I realized
how very much
you meant to me
I can't wait for
you to come back

Dancing
flowers
Pounding
boulders
Beating
waves
Colliding
clouds
Acrobatic
tornado
Thunderous
lightning
Fiery
stars
Shining
moon
Glowing
rainbow
Peaceful
sleep
Dancing
flowers

I
trust you so much
that I am able to
tell you everything
that I feel
and everything
that I think
and be certain that it is
accepted and
understood

I hope
that I may do
the same for you
because it is so vital
to be able to
share oneself
with someone you
trust so much

My trust for you is so complete
You can advise me
You can yell at me
You can be honest with me
But please always tell me
whatever you are thinking
I respect your opinion
as I respect the way you think
and the way you are

You had to go
there is a lot to see
in the world
I had to stay
there is a lot to think about
in the world
I count the time
until we can share our
new experiences with each other
until we can discuss our new
philosophies with each other
I count the time
until we are together again
to share our lives
with each other

Children everywhere
dancing in the streets
their big eyes
searching and innocent
trying to understand life

We must show them love
and be honest with them
We must pursue peace in the world
so that they are free to
find their
dreams

 feel different
from everyone else
I don't need to conform
to what others want me to be
I just need to be what I am
I don't need to impress other people
I just need to do the best I can
I don't need to keep running
I am content with my activities
I don't need a lot of people
I am happy to be alone,
thinking about you
I am very satisfied with my life
I guess it is the knowledge that
though we're not together all the time
you care about everything I do and
you share all my thoughts
and dreams

After ten years
    You are more serious than ever
    You are more honest than ever
    You are more gentle than ever
    You are more interesting than ever
    You are more fun than ever
    You are more creative than ever
    You are more positive than ever
    You are more daring than ever
    You are more sensual than ever
    You are more understanding than ever
    You are more intelligent than ever

After ten years you are more perfect as
    my friend
    my mentor
    my equal
    my partner
    my lover
    than ever

After ten years
        Our love is stronger than ever
        Our love is more tender than ever
        Our love is more honest than ever
        Our love is more overwhelming than ever
        Our love is wilder than ever
        Our love is more exciting than ever
        Our love is more confident than ever
        Our love is more playful than ever
        Our love is more meaningful than ever
After ten years
        Our love is more lasting than ever

Let us
  grow together
  and enrich our lives
  with the friendship
  we share
Let us
  grow together
  and enrich the world
  with the love
  we share

We must adhere to our
own truths before
we are ready to share

If you know yourself well
and have developed a sense
   of confidence
If you are honest with yourself
and honest with others
If you follow your heart
and adhere to your own truths
you are ready to share yourself
you are ready to set goals
you are ready to find happiness
And the more you love
and the more you give
and the more you feel
the more you will receive
from love
and the more you will receive
from life

Where there is honesty
there is understanding
Where there is fairness
there is peace
Where there is sharing
there is friendship
Where there is love
there is fulfillment

There are two types
of creative people.

There are those
who think that their work
is superior to everyone else's.
These people talk about their
work and their art all the time.
They look down on people
for not appreciating their "masterpieces,"
and they are jealous and condescending towards
anyone's work that is accepted.
These creative people are usually
unsuccessful artists
simply because their high opinion of themselves
   and their work
gets in their way.

Then there are those
who think that their work
is important, but
mostly in terms of their own self-satisfaction.
They talk a lot less
and create a lot more than the other type of person.
They work very hard
and they appreciate other people's feelings
towards them and their work.
These creative people are usually
successful artists
because their realistic opinion of themselves
lets them work and grow past obstacles.

Everyone strives for success
   but are they really ready for it?
   Success brings
   self-satisfaction
   respect from society and one's peers
a continual excitement with life
and freedom to live the way you want
But success also brings a
great responsibility for a lot of people—
never ending work to stay successful
never ending pressure to do more
   and be more successful
and a loss of freedom to be irresponsible
Everyone strives for success
but if they are not ready to accept
all that it brings
success
rather than being the answer to one's goals
could be the destruction of one's goals

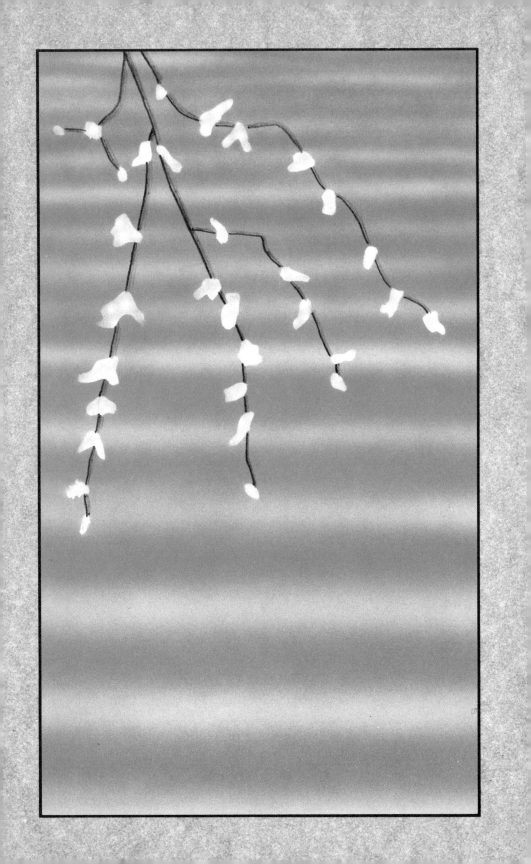

In order to have a successful relationship
you need to put out of your mind
any lessons learned from previous relationships
because if you carry a sensitivity or fear with you
you won't be acting freely
and you won't let yourself be really known

In order to have a successful relationship
it is essential that both people
be completely open and honest

Times have changed and
relationships have changed
We don't need to depend
on each other for everything
We don't need to live our lives
through each other
I am so glad
that we are together, now that
we can be free people
with our own desires
with our own goals
and our own activities
sharing our experiences
our lives
and our
love

The phone rings
    at breakfast
    The phone rings
    while we are showering
    The phone rings
while we are working
The phone rings
at lunch
The phone rings
while we are writing
The phone rings
at dinner
The phone rings
while we are listening to music
The phone rings
while we are making love
The phone rings
while we are on the other phone

I am going to
tear apart all
the wires in the phone
because if I hear
another ring tonight
my head is going
to explode

Everyone is running
  running from work—
  running from crowds—
  running from home—
  running from themselves
However, we have been running too long
there is nowhere else to go
It is time to run towards
ourselves and
each other

 see
a remarkable difference
between the reactions
of men and women
when listening
to me in a work situation
Women are so
much easier
to work with
They listen with respect
to what I say
Many men listen
but try to
ignore what I say
"How can a woman know what to do anyway?" they think.
I then have to repeat myself
and this time it must be in a
more aggressive tone
otherwise they will think that I am weak and unsure
I often find myself frustrated at this point
and overact to counter their attitude
They look at me with a giveaway expression and think
"It's probably that time of the month!"
But when men listen to other men
they listen attentively and rarely question them
As far as we have come
in the world today
it is a constant subconscious fight
at many levels
to work with most men—
Liberated as they are,
they still don't know
how to react to
a woman being in
a higher position
than
they are

Many women
I have talked to lately
tell me that they are
extremely unfulfilled being housewives
that their work all day
is so unimportant
that they are not using
their minds—
These women must
do something that
interests them
but they must also
be reassured that
being a good mother is a
very important job
and that just because society
seems to say that raising children is a menial task
there is no reason to believe this
In fact many beliefs that society
imposes on the individual
are wrong
Women must realize
that whatever they do
is important
as long as they do it well

Today's woman—
strength
tenderness
self-knowledge
self-confidence
mental alertness
sensitivity
body awareness
physical boldness
softness
not afraid
to be
today's woman—
a person
in full control
of herself

It used to be
    that the man worked
    and the woman stayed at home
    The conflict then
    was that the man
would come home
after a long day of socializing and work
wanting only to be quiet and relax
But the woman
after being alone
at home all day
would want to get out of the house
to interact with people and events
Usually the man would have his way
and the woman would be very frustrated
But they were often able to compromise
    on a solution

Now
the man has a career which is important to him
and the woman has a career which is important to her
A conflict sometimes arises when one needs to move to
    another area to get promoted,
but the other needs to stay to continue in his career

If one person's career will suffer
whose career will it be?
And then that person will always resent the other
for that decision
But they cannot compromise on a solution

Another conflict arises when one is doing very well
    in a career
and the other is not
Feelings must be discussed and understood
so that jealousy and competition are
totally eliminated between the couple

With today's gained freedom and equality
there are new and very difficult conflicts between
    men and women
which will need to be worked out
in order for a couple to
happily share
their lives

Some people are
always on an even
path in life

Not me
I'm either very up
or very down
And as long as the ups
outnumber the downs
then it's a very exciting
way to live

When my mind
  feels crazy
  I just watch
  the regularity
  of the ocean waves
and stare at
the steady motion
of the clouds
Spending such peaceful minutes
with nature
has a wonderful
calming
effect

Why do I put you
through such misery
when I love you
so much
Why do I act so moody
with you
when I love you
so much
I must be going through something
which needs a lot of introspection
The only way I'll get over it is
to understand it
and not take it out
on anyone else
especially
you
whom I love
so much

Where are all the people
who enjoyed simple things
who used to go out in the sunlight
and sing songs as they gardened
stopping and talking with
all the neighbors?
Where are all the people
who enjoyed life
who used to consider the home
the most important place to be
and who used to consider the family
the most important people to be with?
Times have changed most of these people
and urged them to seek the complicated
Yet it is only the very basic simple things
in life
that can make people truly
happy

We need to grow—
    to probe
    to learn about ourselves

    We need to grow—
to appreciate others' needs
to share others' feelings

We need to grow—
to experience new things
to learn new things

We need to grow individually
We need to grow together
to understand more about life
to understand more about love

Many people
go from one thing
to another
searching for happiness
But with each new venture
they find themselves
more confused
and less happy
until they discover
that what they are
searching for
is inside themselves
and what will make them happy
is sharing their real selves
with the ones they love

Sharing my life with
those I love
makes my life complete

The love
of a family
is so
uplifting.

The warmth
of a family
is so
comforting.

The support
of a family
is so reassuring.

The attitude
of a family
towards
each other
molds one's
attitude forever
towards the
world.

When we lived
near each other
we participated in
the same activities
Our friendship was
strong
because we shared
so many things
Now—living apart
we rarely
see each other
but our friendship is
even stronger
because we share
the same feelings
This closeness
of hearts
is what makes
a lifetime friendship
like ours

You
so dark and
broad and
masculine
walk hand
in hand
with our little son
so blonde and
slight and
sensitive

Your blue eyes
play with
each other
and I join hands
with both of you
and our laughter
is an echo
of the
songs of birds
and our love
is the sunlight
as we
melt
into
        one
            family

My precious son
four years old
wrote his first
sentence today
He brought it to me—
his eyes glistening—
"Are you proud of
me for doing this?"
he asked
My precious son
I am very proud
of you for writing
a sentence
but I'm even more proud
of you for being
so sensitive
so good
so loving
and so beautiful
I am so proud
that you are
my son
I am so proud
of the love
we share

Rush, Rush
    People running around
    Telephones ringing
    Appointments to keep
    Interviews to grant
Deadlines to meet
It is so reassuring
that in all of this craziness
there is a new life inside my body
struggling so hard
just to grow
a little each day
And I am helping it

reat your child kindly
and it will be kind.

Show your child love every
minute of the day
and it will show love back.

Treat your child gently
and it will be gentle.

Show your child truth
and it will be truthful.

Show your child goodness
and it will be good.

Show your child thoughtfulness
and it will be thoughtful.

Show your child strength
and it will be strong.

Show your child courage
and it will be courageous.

Show your child beauty
and it will be beautiful.

Show your child freedom
and it will be free.

Encourage your child's creativity
and it will be creative.

Encourage your child's sensitivity
and it will be sensitive.

Treat your child special
and it will be a very special person.

My concerned little son
who calls himself "big brother"
to a three-week old fetus
chasing after me with a glass of milk
to drink to make the baby healthy

My caring little son
who reports to his teacher
that a boy is sitting in the corner very sad
He tells the teacher that she
should cheer up the boy

My sensitive little son
who looks in the pond every day
in order to take out any bugs that
might be drowning
who cares about every living
person, animal and flower
as much as he cares about himself

My beautiful little son
whose eyes radiate all the
joy and goodness in his heart
who kisses my hand
and tells me how much he loves me
which is enough love
to carry me
through any day

TWELVE YEARS LATER

Twelve years later
we three
ex-college roommates
who played together
cried together
laughed together
met again
We three
ex-college roommates
knew each other
better than anyone
ever knew us
We lived together through
the most learning years of life
planning our grown-up years
One would marry the best-looking
and happily raise a family
One would marry someone opposite to her family
always hiding and running away from her real self
And one would only marry if she met the very best
and she would strive to be number one herself

Twelve years later
we three
ex-college roommates
met again
We smiled at each other
and it was as if no
time had passed at all
No one looked that different
We were all living the lives that
we had predicted

The only one of us
who really changed
was the one who always wanted
    to be a mother—
a very pretty girl
the center of attraction
She became a wife and
a mother
and during the twelve years
of dedicating her life to her family
she forgot that she was also a person
Her confidence in herself
was lowered
Her image of herself
as an attractive woman
was just a memory

The other was as lovable as ever
and the most fun
but she was still
running around in circles
farther away
from her truths
We always loved this one the most
but always had the feeling that
we wanted to grab her shoulders
and shake some sense into her...

(continued)

...And I who have an exciting but totally different
life than the others (they always said I would)
explained it the best I could
Still serious yet romantic
sensitive and stormy
I mellowed somewhat since college—
no longer throwing
ashtrays at people
no longer needing to be number one
but needing to be at least number two

We laughed
we cried
and understood
each other's
lives as if
we had been
part of each other's lives for the last twelve years
We predicted the next twelve years

One would regain her self-confidence
by pursuing her talents as her children got older

One would be exactly the same
still searching, hiding and having fun

And I would
achieve number two with perseverance

We parted
one for the train
one for the plane
and I to my hotel
So happy to have seen each other
we left with a deeper understanding of ourselves
as can only be seen through real friends
bringing our past into the present
and thinking about this in relationship to the future

Our lives grew so far apart from each other
that we could never again be a part of
    each other's days
But our minds though thinking about different things
shared an understanding of each other that
only friends who live together
at such a growing time in life can
Our own lives—
touched once again
by true friends

I will fill your life with
warmth and
happiness
I will fill your life with
care and
understanding
I will fill your life with
trust and
support
I will fill your life with
friendship and
freedom
I will fill your life with
emotion and
love
I will fill your life with
my experience
my life

E veryone searches for
        love
            They'll tell you that they are not—
                that they are above love
                that love is only in fairy tales
    that love is an emotion only
        weak people have
And until they—
        touch their feelings and
        become honest with themselves
        and show their souls to others
They will be alone—
        alone with no one to share the day's events
        alone in the dark, quiet nights
        alone with no one to understand
        alone with an overwhelmingly painful void
        which can only be filled by
        love
You are the friend I have been searching for—
        I am ready to be completely known
        I am ready to be completely open
        I am ready to share my heart
        I am ready for
        love

Though we are
farther apart
from each other
than ever
we are actually
closer
to each other
than ever
Our activities
and goals
have changed
and our homes
and daily habits
have changed
but we still have the same
souls—
in need of
one another
in need of
our precious
friendship

A friend is
someone who is concerned
with everything you do.

A friend is
someone who is concerned
with everything you think.

A friend is
someone to call upon
during good times.

A friend is
someone to call upon
during bad times.

A friend is
someone who understands
whatever you do.

A friend is
someone who tells the truth
about yourself.

A friend is
someone who knows
what you are going through at all times.

A friend is
someone who refuses to listen
to gossip about you.

A friend is
someone who supports you
at all times.

A friend is
someone who does not
compete with you.

A friend is
someone who is genuinely happy for you
when things go well.

A friend is
someone who tries to cheer you up
when things don't go well.

A friend is
an extension of yourself,
without which
you are not complete.

Thank you for being my friend.

When I am down and out
your presence gives me strength
When I am confused and searching
your presence gives me answers
When I am happy and elated
your presence enables me to share
  my happiness
Please stay forever
in my
life

I want to be able to
        speak the truth
        be a success in my work
        dress the way I want
yet share my days with you

I want to be able to
        enjoy the activities I like
        adhere to my own values
        act the way I feel
yet share my nights with you

I want to be able to
        be myself and
I want you to be able to
        be yourself
yet share our lives with each other

About the Authors

Susan began writing at age seven, and to the delight of millions of readers, she's been writing ever since. Author of five best-selling books of poetry—**Come Into the Mountains, Dear Friend; I Want to Laugh, I Want to Cry; Peace Flows from the Sky; Someone Else to Love** and **Yours If You Ask**—Susan has also authored a collection of her first three books entitled **I'm Not That Kind of Girl** and has an autobiographical novel in-progress.

Susan writes without rhyme, but with all the reason in the world. Expressing her feelings on her natural surroundings, people, love and social change, Susan is endowed with a love of nature and life that she has shared with countless others.

Susan grew up in Peekskill, New York and attended Rider College in New Jersey, earning degrees in English and biology. While doing graduate work in New York City, Susan taught school in Harlem and wrote for numerous magazines and newspapers. A variety of interests and concerns kept her continually involved in new pursuits and constantly finding new outlets for her creativity.

In 1965 Susan met Stephen Schutz. Stephen, a native New Yorker, studied at the New York High School of Music and Art, where he learned the basics of drawing and calligraphy. His great love and appreciation of art became overshadowed by physics books and lab tables at M.I.T. and Princeton University (where he received a Ph.D. degree in theoretical physics in 1970), but it surfaced again when he moved to Colorado for post-doctoral work. Deeply affected by the beauty of his natural surroundings, Stephen decided to give up his career in physics in order to devote all of his time to the development and perfection of his artistic techniques.

Susan and Stephen pursue paths which continually meet, diverge, and meet again. Stephen has illustrated all of Susan's books, as well as designing and illustrating books by other well-known authors. He has also created a line of fine stationery featuring his gentle airbrush blends and has taken beautiful photographs of sunsets which are featured on a unique line of post cards. Stephen studies physics as a hobby.

A special kind of talent is required to translate feelings into poems and emotions into paintings, and Susan and Stephen have that rare gift. It is a gift that has been shared with more than 200 million people around the world. Susan's and Stephen's works have been translated into Spanish, German, and Hebrew, and have been published in Great Britain, Republic of Ireland, Germany, Australia, Argentina, South Africa, the Netherlands and Israel, and distributed in the rest of the nations of the world. In a time of constant fluctuations in social, religious and political standards, Susan's and Stephen's expressions serve to remind us all of our inner spirit and our basic values. As a British newspaper recently commented, "her modern freestyle poems, matched by his artistry, touch the soul."

Photo by Barry Staver

Stephen Schutz

   Stephen Schutz designed and illustrated LOVE, LIVE AND SHARE. His world-wide reputation as an artist comes from the innovative and recognizable style of his airbrushed illustrations and his vivid calligraphy. The adaptability of a scientist to techniques and experiments combined with the sensitivity of an artist to beauty are key factors for Stephen. Stephen's vivid airbrushed blends are described by the media as being "subdued and mystical illustrations designed in harmony with the space of the page and the sentiment of the poem."

   "Each individual printed work is an original print in its own right," Stephen explains, "rather than a reproduction of artwork. The blend of each color and the composition of every component is not finally rendered until the plate is made and the print is lithographed. All factors come into play— the paper colors and the ink mixtures—during the actual printing. I must personally supervise the first printings of all my works."

   Stephen is a "self-contained man." He is an individual who has highly personal convictions. The need for independent growth, challenge and change guides his creativity. Clearly, the originality of his works is reflected in the man, himself.